wild, wild world

WHALES
AND OTHER SEA MAMMALS

Written by
Anita Ganeri

Illustrated by
Ross Watton

p

This is a Parragon Book
First published in 2001

Parragon
Queen Street House
4 Queen Street
Bath BA1 1HE, UK

Copyright © Parragon 2001

Produced by

David West ☆ Children's Books
7 Princeton Court
55 Felsham Road
Putney
London SW15 1AZ

British Library Cataloguing-in-Publication Data

A catalogue record for this book is available from
the British Library.

ISBN 0-75254-667-8

Printed in Italy

Designers
Jenny Skelly
Aarti Parmar
Illustrator
Ross Watton
(SGA)
Cartoonist
Peter Wilks
(SGA)
Editor
James Pickering
Consultant
Steve Parker

CONTENTS

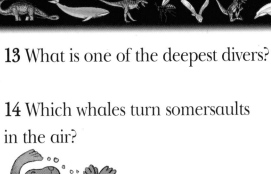

What are sea mammals?

Sea mammals spend most of their lives in or near the sea. There are three groups of sea mammals. Whales and dolphins are called cetaceans. Seals and walruses are called pinnipeds. Manatees and dugongs are called sirenians.

Dugong

4

Amazing! There are well over 10 million crabeater seals living in the icy Antarctic. Seals are found in many parts of the world, but the southern crabeaters are the most common type of seal on Earth.

Blue whale

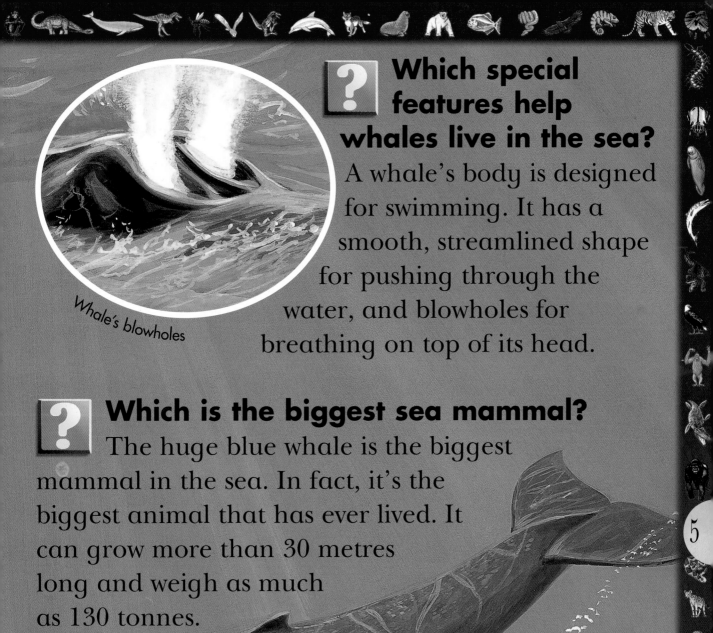

Which special features help whales live in the sea?

A whale's body is designed for swimming. It has a smooth, streamlined shape for pushing through the water, and blowholes for breathing on top of its head.

Whale's blowholes

Which is the biggest sea mammal?

The huge blue whale is the biggest mammal in the sea. In fact, it's the biggest animal that has ever lived. It can grow more than 30 metres long and weigh as much as 130 tonnes.

Is it true?
Whales once lived on land.

Yes. The ancestors of today's whales once lived on land. About 50 million years ago, they went into the sea to look for food and their bodies adapted to life in the water.

Amazing! Whales have a thick layer of fat, called blubber, under their skins. This keeps them warm in the cold sea. At about 50 centimetres, the bowhead whale has the thickest blubber.

? Do all whales have teeth?

Some whales have long, tough bristles, called baleen, hanging down inside their mouths, instead of teeth. They don't chew their food, but sieve it from the water through the baleen.

Baleen whale

Is it true?
A whale uses its blowhole as a nose.

Yes. Like all mammals, whales must breathe air to stay alive. Instead of nostrils, they have a blowhole on top of the head.

6

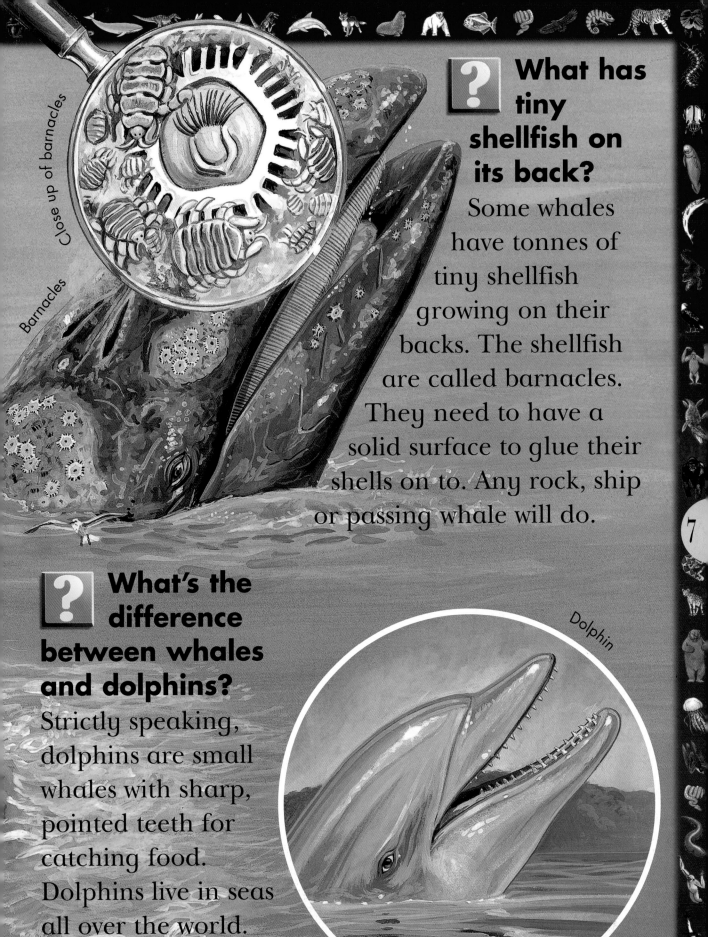

Close up of barnacles

Barnacles

What has tiny shellfish on its back?

Some whales have tonnes of tiny shellfish growing on their backs. The shellfish are called barnacles. They need to have a solid surface to glue their shells on to. Any rock, ship or passing whale will do.

What's the difference between whales and dolphins?

Strictly speaking, dolphins are small whales with sharp, pointed teeth for catching food. Dolphins live in seas all over the world. The biggest dolphin is the killer whale.

Dolphin

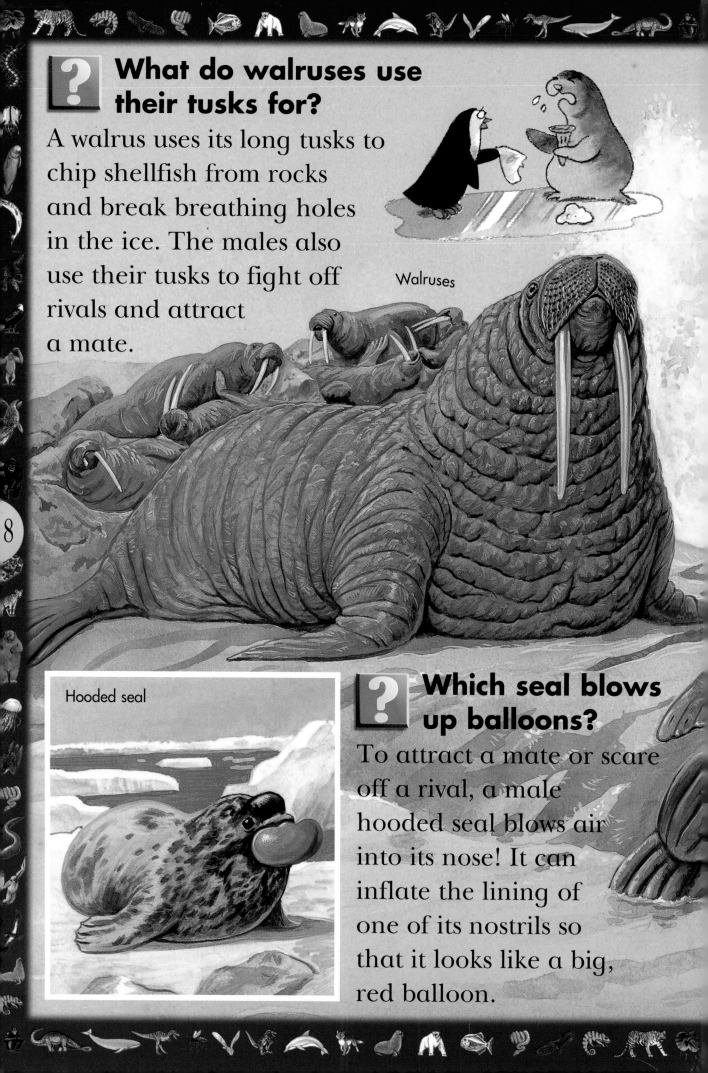

? What do walruses use their tusks for?

A walrus uses its long tusks to chip shellfish from rocks and break breathing holes in the ice. The males also use their tusks to fight off rivals and attract a mate.

Walruses

Hooded seal

? Which seal blows up balloons?

To attract a mate or scare off a rival, a male hooded seal blows air into its nose! It can inflate the lining of one of its nostrils so that it looks like a big, red balloon.

Is it true?

Seals cry when they are sad.

No. Seals sometimes look as if they're crying, but it's not because they're sad. The tears keep their eyes moist and clean. In the sea, they get washed away. On land, they trickle down their cheeks.

Weddell seal

? Which seals live at the ends of the Earth?

Weddell seals live in the far south, on ice-covered islands off the coast of freezing Antarctica. Ringed seals live in the Arctic, at the other end of the world. They've been found as far north as the North Pole.

9

Amazing! In hot weather, some seals and sealions flip tiny pebbles and sand on to their backs with their flippers. This helps to keep them cool, and it also scratches them if their skin is feeling itchy.

? Where do manatees and dugongs live?

Manatees and dugongs live in tropical rivers and in warm, shallow water near the coast, in tropical seas. They are sometimes called 'sea cows' or 'sea pigs' because of their large, lumbering shapes.

Amazing! Florida manatees don't have homes on land, so they sleep on the seabed. They live off the southeastern coast of the United States. These manatees have to come to the surface every ten minutes to breathe the air which keeps them alive.

Dugong

Sea cow

Is it true?
You can tell a dugong's age from its tusks.

Yes. To tell a dugong's age, you need to count the growth rings in its tusks. In the wild, dugongs can live for between 60 and 70 years.

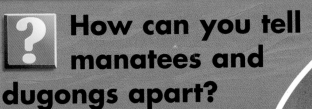

? How can you tell manatees and dugongs apart?

You can tell manatees and dugongs apart by the shape of their tails. A manatee's tail has rounded tips. A dugong's tail has pointed tips, like a dolphin's tail.

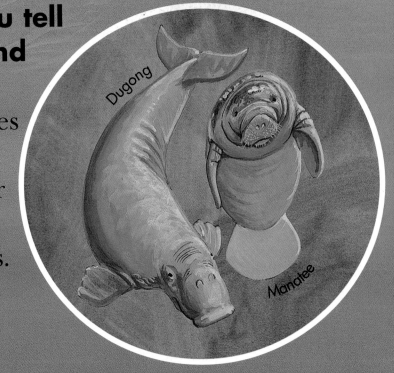

Dugong

Manatee

? Which sea mammals are vegetarians?

Only manatees and dugongs are vegetarians. They feed on sea grasses and other sea plants. They use their bristly lips for pulling up plants. Dugongs also dig up roots from the seabed using their horseshoe-shaped snouts. All other sea mammals eat meat, or other creatures of some kind.

11

? Which sea mammal can swim the fastest?

The fastest sea mammal in the world is the killer whale. With its streamlined body and powerful tail, it can speed through the water at up to 55 kph. That's more than six times faster than the quickest human swimmers.

Killer whales

12

Is it true?
Spinner dolphins spin like tops in the air.

Yes. Spinner dolphins are easy to recognise. They can leap out of the water, high into the air, then spin around quickly like tops. These amazing acrobats live near the coast in warm seas.

Sea lion

Which is the speediest seal?

The fastest seal in the sea is the California sea lion, with a top speed of 40 kph. The fastest on land is the crabeater seal, reaching 19 kph over snow and ice.

Amazing! Some sea mammals can hold their breath for almost two hours before they have to come to the surface for air. Most humans can only hold their breath for a minute or so.

13

Sperm whale

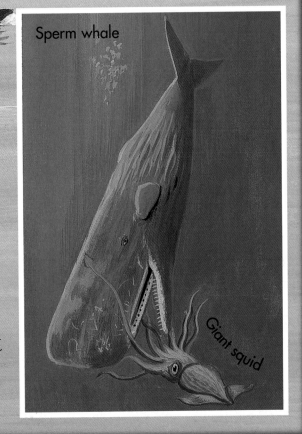

Giant squid

What is one of the deepest divers?

Sperm whales dive over two kilometres after their food. One sperm whale was even found with two deep-sea sharks in its stomach. It must have dived to three kilometres to catch them.

Which whales turn somersaults in the air?

Humpback whales are very athletic. Even though the whales may weigh 65 tonnes, they can leap high into the air and come crashing down into the water on their backs. They can even turn somersaults in the air.

Humpback whale

Amazing! In the Arctic and Antarctic, seals dive under the ice to search for food. They can hold their breath for up to 30 minutes before they need to come up for air, so they chew breathing holes in the ice with their strong front teeth.

Which sea mammals walk with their teeth?

A walrus's tusks are actually its two upper teeth. They grow up to a metre long. The walrus uses its tusks to pull itself out of the sea and drag itself across the land.

Walrus

Grey whale

15

❓ Which sea mammals make the longest journey?

Grey whales spend the summers feeding in the Arctic. In winter, they swim to the coast of Mexico to breed. They swim back north again in the spring, a round trip of about 20,000 kilometres.

Is it true?
Whales slap their tails against the sea surface because they're angry.

No. Some whales slap their huge tails down on the water but it's not because they're angry. This is called 'lobtailing' and it's probably a signal to other whales.

Which are the most intelligent sea mammals?

Dolphins are quick to learn tricks and remember instructions. This makes them very popular with people. They are also friendly and sociable. Many dolphins live in large groups. They play and hunt for food together.

Which seal has a huge nose?

The male northern elephant seal gets its name from its very long nose, which normally hangs down over its mouth. It can inflate its nose, like a balloon, to attract a mate.

Northern elephant seal

Is it true?
Beluga whales are called 'sea canaries' because of their yellow skin.

No. Beluga whales whistle and chirp just like singing birds, such as canaries. In fact, they make so much noise, they're nicknamed 'sea canaries'. Adult belugas have pure white skin.

Dolphin

Humpback whales

17

Amazing! Blue whales' voices are louder than the sound of a jet plane taking off, and can be heard over 500 kilometres away. As well as being the biggest animals, blue whales are the noisiest creatures in the world!

? **Why do whales sing to each other?**

Whales build sounds into 'songs' which can last for ten minutes or more. The whales sing to keep in touch with each other, to find a mate and to frighten off rivals.

Baleen

? Which whale has the longest 'teeth'?

All of the great whales, such as the blue whale have hundreds of bony baleen, which they use to sieve food from the water. The Bowhead whale's baleen are up to four metres long.

Is it true?
Leopard seals are fussy eaters.

No. Leopard seals eat almost anything, including penguins, sea birds, fish, squid, seal pups, and even duck-billed platypuses!

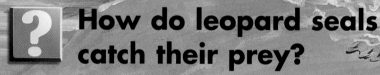

? How do leopard seals catch their prey?

Leopard seals mainly eat penguins. To catch them, the seals build up speed in the water, then launch themselves on to the ice. They have even been known to snap at human divers, probably because they mistake them for penguins.

Blue whale

Which sea mammal has the biggest appetite?

Blue whales have massive appetites. In spring and summer, they eat up to four tonnes of krill (tiny, shrimp-like creatures) each day. That's about five times as much food as you eat each year!

Leopard seal

Amazing! Whales and dolphins can shut off their windpipes when they're underwater. They do this when they're feeding. It stops water from passing into their lungs and making them choke.

19

What finds food with its whiskers?

A walrus has a thick moustache of about 600 whiskers around its snout. It uses them to feel for shellfish, sea urchins, fish and crabs on the seabed.

Walrus

Which sea mammals use fishing nets?

Humpbacks, killer whales and dolphins swim around shoals of fish, blowing bubbles from their blowholes. Then they swim and gobble the trapped fish up!

 Amazing! Some seals swallow stones and pebbles. No one knows exactly why. Perhaps, like some birds which do the same, they swallow the stones to help grind up their food, or maybe they stop hunger pangs.

Yes. Dolphins use sound to find food underwater. They make clicking sounds which are too high-pitched for human ears to hear. If the sounds hit a solid object, like a fish, they send back echoes. From the echoes, the dolphins can tell what's nearby.

Humpback whale

21

Dolphins hunting fish

What uses a ceiling of water to catch fish?

When dolphins are hunting for anchovy, they herd the fish towards the surface of the water, giving them one less direction of escape. They also make loud noises, which might confuse the fish, making them easier to catch.

Amazing! Walruses get sunburnt. Walruses are usually brown. But in strong sun, their blood flows to the skin's surface to soak up the heat. This can turn the walruses' skin a bright shade of pink.

Killer whales

? How can you tell humpback whales apart?

Humpback whales have special black and white markings under their tails. Each whale has its own particular pattern which can be used to tell the whales apart. These markings are unique to each whale, just like one person's fingerprints are never the same as anybody else's.

Humpback whale

? Why are killer whales black and white?

The killer whale's black and white colouring looks very striking, but it could be camouflage. It might help to hide the whale among the light and shade near the water surface, so it can take fish and seals by surprise.

23

? Which whales change colour as they grow up?

Beluga whales live in the Arctic Ocean. New-born beluga babies are reddish-brown in colour. After about a year, their skin changes colour to grey. When they're five years old, they turn pure white.

Beluga whales

Which are the biggest sea mammal babies?

When a baby blue whale is born, it weighs between two and three tonnes. It drinks about 200 litres of its mother's milk a day, and by seven months old, it weighs 20 tonnes!

Blue whale and calf

Which sea mammals live in a pod?

Some dolphins live in family groups called pods. A pod may be hundreds of dolphins strong. The dolphins help each other out. If one of them is ill, for example, the others look after it, by pushing it to the surface so that it can breathe.

Which sea mammals live the longest?

Whales and dolphins have long lives. Fin whales probably live the longest, between 90 and 100 years. The Baird's beaked whale is close behind. It can live for up to 80 years.

Fin whale

Pod of dolphins

Is it true?
Baby whales and dolphins are born head first.

No. A baby whale or dolphin is born tail first. Otherwise it might drown. Its mother pushes it to the surface so that it can take its first breath.

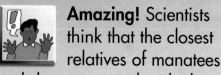

Amazing! Scientists think that the closest relatives of manatees and dugongs may be elephants! After all, they're all large and lumbering, they're all greyish in colour and they all eat plants. But they drifted apart millions of years ago.

Pilot whales

Dugongs

? Why do whales get stranded on the beach?

Groups of whales sometimes get stranded on the shore. If they can't return to the sea, they die. No one knows why this happens. It may be because they're ill, or get confused and lose their way.

Is it true?
Narwhals use their tusks for jousting.

Yes. Only male narwhals grow long, spiralling tusks. It is thought that they may use their tusks as jousting weapons to fight off rival narwhals for a mate.

Narwhals

❓ Do unicorns really exist?

Not on land, but people used to hunt narwhals, a type of whale, and sell their tusks as unicorn horns. The tusk is the narwhal's tooth. It grows up to 2.5 metres long.

❓ Which sea mammals did sailors mistake for mermaids?

The legend of the mysterious mermaid may have started with a dugong. Close-to, dugongs don't look anything like mermaids, but from a distance, and in a sea mist, they do look a bit like human shapes, complete with fish-like tails.

? **Which seal pups were hunted for their coats?**

Harp seal pups are born with soft, white fur coats. They lose these after a month and grow dark coats like adult seals. In the past, thousands of pups were killed for their fur.

28

Amazing! Steller's sea cows were huge dugongs that once lived in the Bering Sea. They were discovered in 1741. Just 30 years later, they were extinct because so many had been eaten by sailors.

Why are sea mammals in danger?

People are very dangerous for sea mammals. They hunt seals and whales for their meat, fur and blubber, and they trap sea mammals, such as dolphins, in fishing nets. Many more mammals are poisoned by pollution, such as oil from tankers, which is dumped into the sea.

Is it true?
Right whales are easy to hunt.

Yes. Right whales were once the right whales to hunt. They swam slowly and floated on the surface when they were killed.

29

Whale hunt

Gulf porpoises

Which are the rarest sea mammals?

There are fewer than 600 Mediterranean monk seals left, but the rarest sea mammal is probably the Gulf porpoise. There may be only 50 left off the Californian coast.

Elephant seal

30

Amazing! Most whales and dolphins are able to snooze for a few minutes while they're swimming or resting on the sea floor. But it's thought that the Dall's porpoise never goes to sleep at all.

? Which is the biggest seal?

Antarctic southern elephant seals are the biggest seals. Male seals grow up to six metres long, measure almost four metres around the middle and weigh in at about three tonnes.

Blue whale

Is it true? *Sperm whales have the heaviest mammal brains.*

Yes. A sperm whale's brain weighs up to nine kilograms. That's about six times heavier than a human brain! Luckily, the whale has a very large head to fit it in, which takes up about a third of its body.

Which whale is the tiniest?

The smallest whale is probably the Commerson's dolphin. This miniature mammal grows about one metre long. It would take about 3,000 dolphins to make up the weight of one blue whale.

Commerson's dolphin

Which whale has the tallest "blow"?

The 'blow' is the spout of water you see when a whale breathes out. The gigantic blue whale has the tallest blow. It can reach a height of twelve metres, as high as six tall people. Each whale makes a different pattern as it blows.

Glossary

Baleen Long, tough bristles hanging down inside some whales' mouths. They are used for sieving food from the sea. Only great whales, such as the blue whale have baleen.

Barnacles Tiny shellfish which grow on rocks and the bottom of ships. Barnacles also stick to whales' backs.

Blowhole The hole on top of a whale's head which it uses for breathing out.

Blubber A thick layer of fat under a sea mammal's skin, which protects it from the cold.

Camouflage A special colouring or pattern on the surface of an animal, which makes it blend in with its background, making it difficult to see, and less likely to be attacked by another animal.

Echo-location The way that some animals use sound to locate food and find their way around. They make sounds which hit solid objects and send back echoes. From these, the animals can tell what the objects are, and where they are.

Krill Tiny, shrimp-like sea creatures. Huge amounts of krill are eaten by whales every day.

Lobtailing When whales slap their tails on the surface of the sea, as a signal to other whales.

Mammals The group of animals which gives birth to live young, look after their babies and feed them on milk.

Pods The name for family groups of dolphins, seals and whales.

32

Index